OUR GOVERNMENT

Vice President

by Kirsten Chang

BELLWETHER MEDIA • MINNEAPOLIS, MN

Blastoff! Readers are carefully developed by literacy experts to build reading stamina and move students toward fluency by combining standards-based content with developmentally appropriate text.

Level 1 provides the most support through repetition of high-frequency words, light text, predictable sentence patterns, and strong visual support.

Level 2 offers early readers a bit more challenge through varied sentences, increased text load, and text-supportive special features.

Level 3 advances early-fluent readers toward fluency through increased text load, less reliance on photos, advancing concepts, longer sentences, and more complex special features.

★ **Blastoff! Universe**

Reading Level

Grade **K**

Grades **1–3**

Grade **4**

This edition first published in 2021 by Bellwether Media, Inc.

No part of this publication may be reproduced in whole or in part without written permission of the publisher. For information regarding permission, write to Bellwether Media, Inc., Attention: Permissions Department, 6012 Blue Circle Drive, Minnetonka, MN 55343.

Library of Congress Cataloging-in-Publication Data

Names: Chang, Kirsten, 1991- author.
Title: Vice president / by Kirsten Chang.
Description: Minneapolis, MN : Bellwether Media, 2021. | Series: Blastoff! readers. Our government | Includes bibliographical references and index.| Audience: Ages 5-8 | Audience: Grades K-1 | Summary: "Developed by literacy experts for students in kindergarten through grade three, this book introduces the vice president to young readers through leveled text and related photos"–Provided by publisher.
Identifiers: LCCN 2019059260 (print) | LCCN 2019059261 (ebook) | ISBN 9781644872062 (library binding) | ISBN 9781681038308 (paperback) | ISBN 9781618919649 (ebook)
Subjects: LCSH: Vice presidents–United States–Juvenile literature.
Classification: LCC JK609.5 .C53 2021 (print) | LCC JK609.5 (ebook) | DDC 352.23/90973–dc23
LC record available at https://lccn.loc.gov/2019059260
LC ebook record available at https://lccn.loc.gov/2019059261

Editor: Rebecca Sabelko   Designer: Laura Sowers

Printed in the United States of America, North Mankato, MN.

Table of Contents

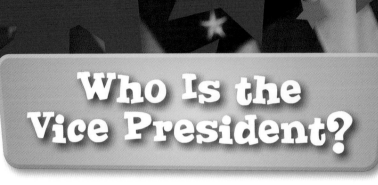

Who Is the Vice President?

The United States vice president is **second-in-command**. This person may be called VP.

Vice President Mike Pence

President Donald Trump

The VP is in the **executive branch**.

Working Together

Legislative Branch	Executive Branch	Judicial Branch
writes laws	signs laws	studies laws

president

vice president

Senate   House of Representatives   Supreme Court

People **elect**
the VP along
with the president.
They serve four years.

Must Haves

- ✓ **35 or older**
- ✓ **born in U.S.**
- ✓ **citizen at least 14 years**

**Vice President
George H. W. Bush
in 1985**

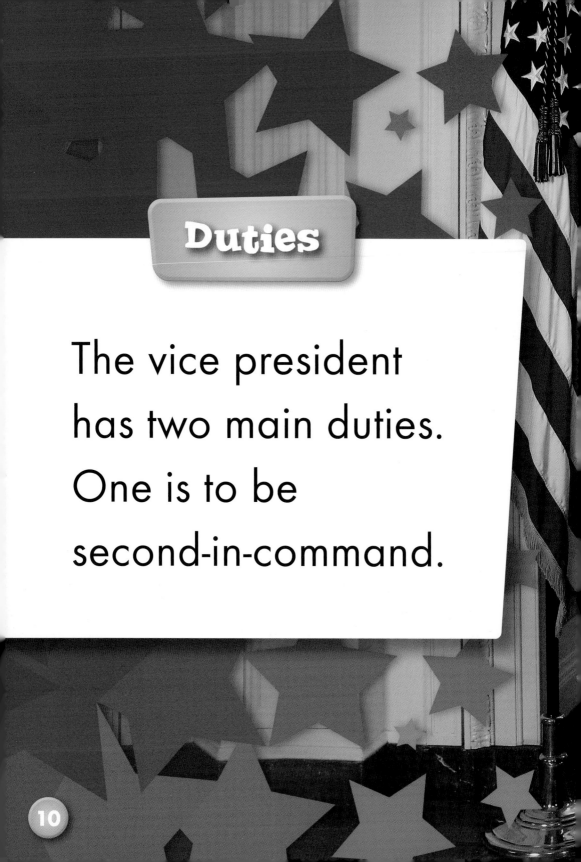

Duties

The vice president has two main duties. One is to be second-in-command.

**Vice President
Joe Biden**

**President
Barack Obama**

The other duty is to be head of the **Senate**.

Vice President
Al Gore

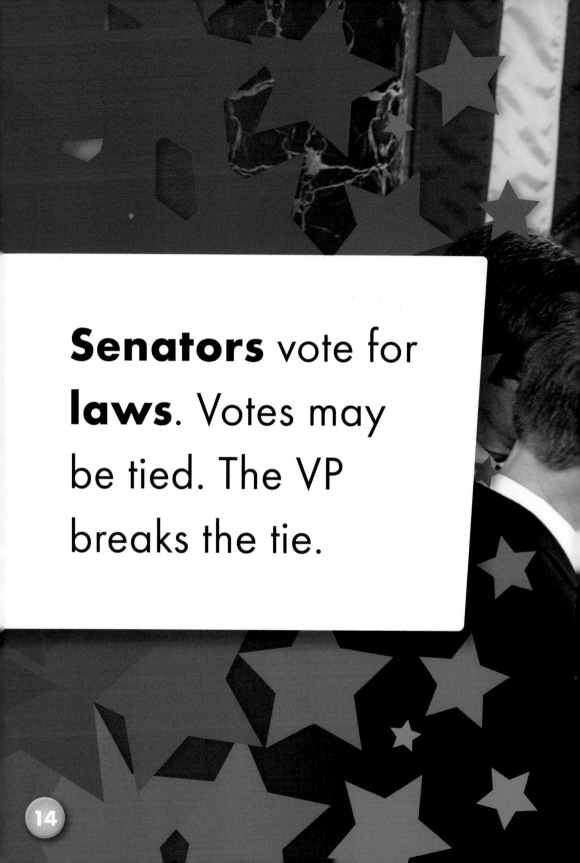

Senators vote for **laws**. Votes may be tied. The VP breaks the tie.

Vice President
Dick Cheney

An Important Job

The president
has a hard job.
They can ask
the VP for help.

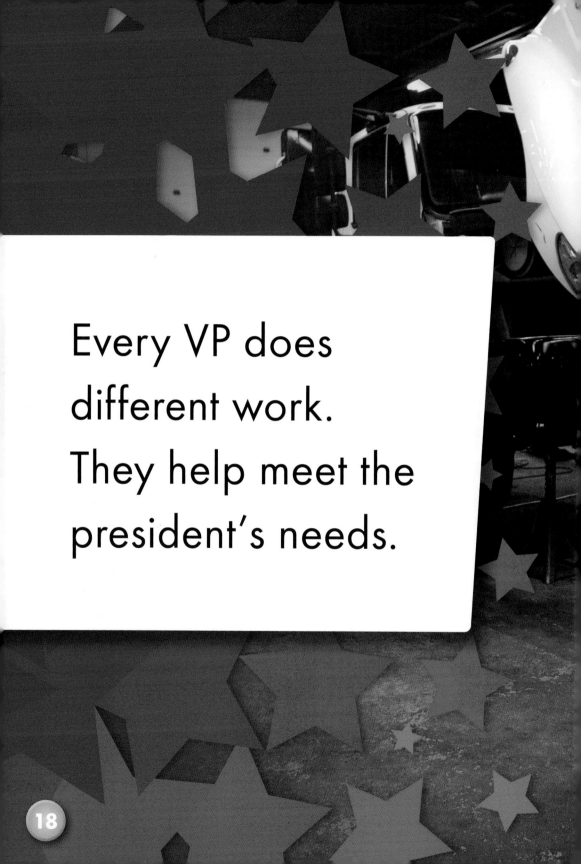

Every VP does different work. They help meet the president's needs.

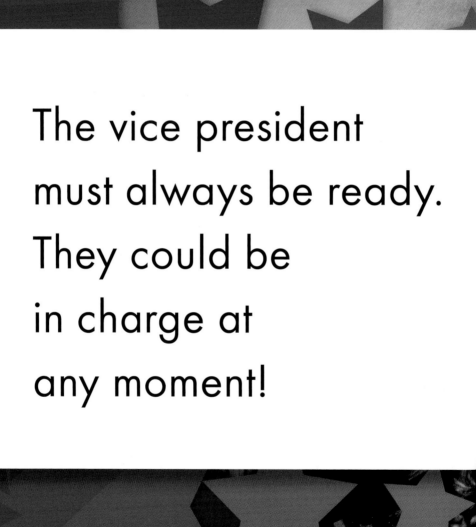

The vice president
must always be ready.
They could be
in charge at
any moment!

How would I prepare to lead?

Vice President Lyndon B. Johnson becomes president

Glossary

elect

to vote for someone to be a leader

second-in-command

the person who leads if anything happens to the current leader

executive branch

the part of government that makes sure laws are followed

Senate

a part of the legislative branch; the Senate makes laws.

laws

rules that people must follow

senators

members of the Senate; there are 100 United States senators.

To Learn More

AT THE LIBRARY

Bonwill, Ann. *We Have a Government.* New York, N.Y.: Children's Press, 2019.

Murray, Julie. *Vice President.* Minneapolis, Minn.: Abdo Kids, 2018.

Schuh, Mari. *The Senate.* Minneapolis, Minn.: Bellwether Media, 2021.

ON THE WEB

FACTSURFER

Factsurfer.com gives you a safe, fun way to find more information.

1. Go to www.factsurfer.com.

2. Enter "vice president" into the search box and click 🔍.

3. Select your book cover to see a list of related content.

Index

The images in this book are reproduced through the courtesy of: Joseph Sohm, front cover (podium); Everett Collection Inc/ Alamy, pp. 4-5; Andriy Blokhin, pp. 6-7; Hum Historical/ Alamy, pp. 8-9; dpa picture alliance/ Alamy, pp. 10-11; New York Daily News Archive/ Getty, pp. 12-13; Mark Wilson/ Getty, pp. 14-15; ZUMA Press, Inc./ Alamy, pp. 16-17; WDC Photos/ Alamy, pp. 18-19; IanDagnall Computing/ Alamy, pp. 20-21; vchal, p. 22 (elect); Joe Sohm, p. 22 (executive branch); Freedomz, p. 22 (laws); a katz, p. 22 (second-in-command); mark reinstein, p. 22 (Senate); US Senate/ Alamy, p. 22 (senators).

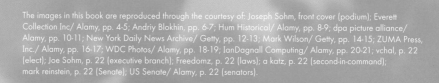